Daily *warm-ups*

WRITING

J. WESTON
WALCH
PUBLISHER
Portland, Maine

1   2   3   4   5   6   7   8   9   10
ISBN 0-8251-4485-X
Copyright © 2003
J. Weston Walch, Publisher
P.O. Box 658 • Portland, Maine 04104-0658
www.walch.com
Printed in the United States of America

The *Daily Warm-Ups* series is a wonderful way to turn extra classroom minutes into valuable learning time. The 180 quick activities—one for each day of the school year—review, practice, and teach writing skills. These daily activities may be used at the very beginning of class to get students into learning mode, near the end of class to make good educational use of that transitional time, in the middle of class to shift gears between lessons—or whenever else you have minutes that now go unused. In addition to providing students with structure and focus, they are a natural path to other classroom activities involving writing skills. As students build their vocabularies and become more adept at composition, they will be better prepared for standardized tests, such as the PSAT and SAT.

Daily Warm-Ups are easy-to-use reproducibles—simply photocopy the day's activity and distribute it. Or make a transparency of the activity and project it on the board. You may want to use the activities for extra credit points or as a check on the writing skills that are built and acquired over time.

However you choose to use them, *Daily Warm-Ups* are a convenient and useful supplement to your regular lesson plans. Make every minute of your class time count!

Writing is one of the abilities that sets humankind apart from other animals. In China, Japan, and some Islamic cultures, writing can be an art form: calligraphy. In ancient Egypt, papyrus, a paperlike medium, was invented so that people would have something portable to write on.

Writing has a fascinating history, yet it is something we often take for granted. Think about writing in your daily life. Jot down all the types of writing you do in a typical day.

Now write a few sentences about what your life would be like if you were unable to write. Share your ideas with classmates.

1

Do you remember what a haiku is? It is a very controlled type of poem, usually about nature. It has three lines with the following syllable pattern: five syllables, seven syllables, five syllables. A haiku tries to capture the feeling of a moment, and it contains a season reference. Read the haiku below.

Bright green leaves bud out
A promise of blooms to come
Part of the cycle

Write a haiku about the end of summer.

2

Make a list of all the words you think of when you hear the word *school*. Then write a sentence, using some of those words, that sums up your overall feelings about school.

3

Communication plays a big part in life. When someone has the option of speaking or writing, when does he or she choose the latter? List the circumstances or situations in which writing is preferable to speaking, and why. Then see if classmates generated similar lists.

4

Whenever you learn or practice a skill, it is a good idea to keep some basics in mind. Let's review some grammar. Do you remember the parts of speech? There are eight. List as many as you can below. Then write an example of each.

5

A noun is a word that names a person, a place, an object, or an idea. Nouns can be common or proper; that is, they can name any object, or a very specific object. For example, *teacher* is a common noun. *Mr. Hernandez* is a proper noun. Proper nouns are always capitalized.

List five common nouns that name someone or something you see every day.

Now list five proper nouns that name someone or something you see every day.

What does including proper nouns (besides names of characters) do for a piece of writing? How does it help the reader?

6

Pronouns are words that take the place of nouns.

Personal pronouns include *I*, *we*, *you*, *he*, *she*, *they*, and *it*.

Fill in the blanks with the appropriate personal pronoun from the list above.

1. _____ ate breakfast before _____ brushed my teeth.

2. Jack borrowed my CD, but _____ never returned it.

3. Tyrone gave Jeanie a pencil, but _____ would have preferred a pen.

4. Alexander gave Lizzie his pencil because _____ prefers pens.

Look back at your answers. How did you know which pronouns to write? How can you ensure that you use the correct pronouns in your writing?

7

© 2003 J. Weston Walch, Publisher

Possessive pronouns show possession, or ownership.

These are also a kind of personal pronoun. Possessive pronouns include *my, mine, our, ours, your, yours, his, hers, its,* and *theirs.* Rewrite the following paragraph using personal pronouns in place of some of the nouns.

Esmeralda loved playing Esmeralda's clarinet. Although Esmeralda was talented, Esmeralda lacked the discipline to practice every day. Esmeralda's dream was to play professionally. Esmeralda's parents worried that Esmeralda's parents' daughter would not reach Esmeralda's goal if Esmeralda did not work harder.

8

Verbs are words that show action or state of being. *Run, walk, chew, study,* and *sleep* are all verbs. *Am, is, was, have, do,* and *own* are verbs, too.

Make a list of ten verbs that describe some action you have engaged in today. Choose verbs more interesting than forms of *to be*!

Adjectives are words that describe nouns or pronouns. Adjectives add detail and interest to writing.

Insert at least five adjectives in the paragraph below. Make other changes if necessary.

Justin wrote an essay about his vacation. It was three pages long. His topic was broad enough to fill the space, but it was not very interesting. It would have been more fun to read if he had described the people he met, the places he saw, and the things he did. Instead, he just talked about the things he ate.

Which version of the paragraph do you prefer—with or without adjectives? Why?

Daily Warm-Ups: Writing

10

Adjectives help make a description more specific and real to the reader. Adjectives can appeal to any of the senses to help the reader experience what the writer is talking about.

Choose an object in your classroom. Write one adjective for each of the five senses (sight, hearing, taste, smell, touch) to describe that object. Then exchange lists with a classmate and see if you can guess each other's object.

11

Descriptions often rely on the sense of sight. But you have four other senses you can draw on to create images for your readers.

The sense of smell is considered our most nostalgic sense; particular smells can conjure up scenes from the past. Think about a scent that has some meaning or association for you. Then describe the scent and the feelings it brings up.

Daily Warm-Ups: Writing

12

The sense of touch is one that is often overlooked.

You can appeal to the sense of touch by describing an object's temperature, heaviness or lightness, and texture, for example. Telling what kind of material something is made of also helps with a touch image.

Write a description of one of the following items, appealing to the sense of touch:

- a paperback book
- your favorite food
- a fun sport

The sense of taste is one that is used only occasionally in descriptions, because you only taste a limited number of things. Think of something that you would not normally eat but that would not be harmful to taste. Describe that item (without actually tasting it). For example, a rock might taste metallic and earthy, or a tire might taste of oil and tar.

Daily Warm-Ups: Writing

14

Think about an object or quality unique to the area where you live. Imagine that you work for a travel agency, and you are writing a brochure to attract visitors to your area. Write a description of the unique object or quality to include in your brochure.

15

Adverbs, like adjectives, modify other words. Some adverbs modify verbs; for example, *he snored **loudly***. Other adverbs modify adjectives, as in *his snore was **very** loud*. Some adverbs modify other adverbs. *He snored **quite** loudly* is an example.

Write a paragraph about a hobby, sport, or interest of yours. Explain how you do this activity, using at least three adverbs.

When you have finished, cross out the adverbs in your paragraph, and read the paragraph to yourself. What do you think of the paragraph with no adverbs? Do you prefer the paragraph with adverbs, or without? Why?

16

Part of writing well is using vocabulary correctly.

Which sentence is correct?

    a. I will have to altar my plans if I want to go to the concert.

    b. He altered his suit after he took up body building.

The answer is b. *Altar* and *alter* are a pair of often confused words. There are many such words in English. For each pair of sentences below, circle the letter of the correct sentence. If you are not sure which is correct, check a dictionary.

1. a. Susan sat down on the steps and began to cry.

    b. Ella set down next to her to find out what was wrong.

2. a. He set his book too close to the fire.

    b. Then he set and stared at the charred remains.

3. a. Beth raised her hand in class.

    b. The elephant rose its trunk in greeting.

4. a. The flames rose from the dry wood.

    b. The smoke raised in billowing clouds.

17

© 2003 J. Weston Walch, Publisher

On her way to the gym, the dog chased Maria.

The sentence above suggests that the dog was sidetracked on her way to the canine fitness center by a tempting target. The meaning of the sentence could be made clearer by moving the modifier closer to what it is modifying: *On her way to the gym, Maria was chased by the dog.* Another way to fix the sentence is to reword it: *Maria was on her way to the gym when the dog chased her.*

Rewrite the following sentences to clarify or change the meaning.

1. While driving to the store, the dog slobbered on his owner's jacket.

2. The skiers swooshed past the lodge blinded by the storm.

3. He said he would go first, then he changed his mind and stayed home.

4. Before finishing her rounds, Suzanne asked the doctor for some advice.

Daily Warm-Ups: Writing

18

"This is the way the world ends

Not with a bang but with a whimper."

—T. S. Eliot, "The Hollow Men"

These poetic lines use onomatopoeia. Onomatopoeia refers to words that come from sounds.

What do you think of the image in the poem? What do you think Eliot means?

Which of the following sentences gives you a stronger image?

The rain plashed into the birdbath.

The rain fell into the birdbath.

The first sentence uses onomatopoeia (words that sound like sounds) to give the reader a clear auditory (sound) image. *Crash, slam, trill,* and *clatter* are all examples of onomatopoeia.

Write three sentences of your own using onomatopoeia. The three sentences have to be the same, except for the onomatopoeia. For example, besides the two sentences at the top of the page, you might write *The rain splooshed into the birdbath* or *The rain tinkled into the birdbath.* Each sentence gives a different image.

20

Rewrite the following paragraph using onomatopoeia.

The boat moved through the water. The air was heavy. Birds called, and unseen creatures moved into the water. Stinging bugs flew around the boat. Suddenly, Jack heard something traveling in the dense bushes. He stifled a call when the thing came through the leaves onto the river bank. It was just his dog, Buddy!

Onomatopoeia is one device writers use to create sound images. Writers also use other devices to create sensory images. These devices are called figurative language.

One common type of figurative language is the simile. A simile makes a comparison between two unlike things, using *like* or *as*. As *hot as an oven*, *as cold as ice*, and *ate like a pig* are all examples of similes, although they are not very original ones.

Write three interesting similes related to something you have done or will do today.

22

Complete the similes below.

Make them as interesting, unusual, or as surprising as you can. Just make sure they still make sense and give a clear image.

1. as bright as a(n) _____

2. as _____ as a rabbit's foot

3. as worthless as a(n) _____

4. like a(n) _____ after dark

5. like a(n) _____ in a downpour

23

© 2003 J. Weston Walch, Publisher

Similes are one type of figurative language.
Metaphors are another. Metaphors, like similes, make a comparison
between two unlike things. Unlike similes, however, metaphors do
not use the words *like* or *as*.

She fought like a lion is a simile.

She was a lion in battle is a metaphor.

Write three metaphors about something you do outside of school.

24

Columbus Day is celebrated to commemorate Christopher Columbus's discovery of America. Of course, he did not exactly discover it; there were already people living here. Write a dialogue between two native people who have just seen Columbus's men coming ashore. One person has never seen European explorers before; the other has.

25

Personification is a literary device that gives human attributes to a nonhuman object. For example, *the wind whined in the leafless trees* is personification. Wind does not really whine; people (unfortunately) do. Using personification makes nonhuman things seem as though they have the abilities and the will that people have, giving a strong image of what the writer is describing.

Describe something using personification. Then share your sentence with a classmate to get feedback on your image.

26

Hyperbole, or overstatement, is a literary device that uses exaggeration. Someone who describes the cafeteria line as "twenty miles long" is using hyperbole. Think about examples of hyperbole you have heard, whether in personal conversation, on television, in the newspaper, or in some other kind of communication. In what kind of situation does someone use hyperbole?

27

Hyperbole can sometimes be used to humorous effect. Write three examples of hyperbole that create humorous images.

28

The opposite of hyperbole is understatement.

With hyperbole, someone exaggerates to the extreme. With understatement, someone plays down what he or she is describing.

For example, imagine that Tyler turns red, throws his books into his locker, and slams the door so hard that the whole line of lockers rattles. An observer comments, "Tyler is a little upset." That person is using understatement.

Think about situations in which you have heard understatement used. When do people use this device? Why?

29

Rewrite the paragraph below, using hyperbole.

Then rewrite the paragraph again, using understatement. Make any other necessary changes. When you have finished, share and discuss your paragraphs with a classmate. Which one did he or she prefer? Why?

Hannah rode her bike to school. She stowed it in the rack. She was late, so she ran to homeroom, a clear violation of hallway policy. When she got there she found that she was later than she had thought; the lunch bell rang.

30

An allusion is a reference to something from a well-known source, such as the Bible, mythology, literature, or historical events. For example, if someone is described as having a Jekyll-and-Hyde personality, he or she has two opposite personalities, one good and one evil. This is an allusion to Robert Louis Stevenson's novel *The Strange Case of Dr. Jekyll and Mr. Hyde*. And if you call someone a Benedict Arnold, you are probably calling him or her a traitor.

Can you think of any allusions you have come across, perhaps in books you have read? Write them down. Then explain what you think allusion adds to a piece of writing.

31

Write a sentence using an allusion. Your reference may be to persons, things, or events from the Bible, mythology, literature, or history, or it may be an allusion to something familiar to you and your classmates, such as a school event.

32

The following words are often misused. On the line next to each vocabulary word, write the letter of the correct definition from the box. If you are not sure of a meaning, check the dictionary.

a. to receive

b. other than

c. to offer counsel

d. suggestion for action

e. to influence; to act on

f. result

g. a thing used for a specific function

h. to invent

i. spectacle; view

j. location

___ 1. accept

___ 2. advise

___ 3. affect

___ 4. sight

___ 5. device

___ 6. devise

___ 7. advice

___ 8. except

___ 9. site

___ 10. effect

Part of writing well is using the mechanics of writing correctly. You might have great ideas, but if you cannot follow the standard conventions, people may have difficulty understanding your message. Punctuation is intended to make writing easier to understand.

Do you know how to use commas? Write three comma rules below. Then give an example of each.

34

Insert the commas needed in the paragraph below.

Once in a while Sheila went to the movies alone. She didn't have to share her popcorn she didn't have to shush her companion and she didn't have to debate which movie to see. On the other hand there was also no one to poke in the ribs when a character said something funny and there was no one to explain when something unexpected happened. She wasn't sure which way was better but she loved going to the movies.

Daily Warm-Ups: Writing

35

Write three rules for when to use a period. Give one example of each.

36

Insert periods where they are needed in the following sentences.

1. Take W River St to Overpass Rd, and turn left at the first set of lights

2. Miss Washington is my piano teacher this year

3. Dr Ahmed ordered some tests to be done at the lab on E 42nd Street

4. It's impossible that M L Burns is Melissa Lou Burns

5. I have a copy of *The Elements of Style* by William Strunk, Jr, and E B White

37

© 2003 J. Weston Walch, Publisher

Question marks are used at the end of interrogative sentences, or questions. *How much does that car cost?* and *Is it safe to drink the water?* use question marks.

A question mark is not used at the end of an indirect question. *He asked how much the car cost* and *They wondered if it was safe to drink the water* would end with periods, not question marks.

Change the periods to question marks where appropriate.

1. Twinkle, twinkle, little star, how I wonder what you are.

2. How much is that doggie in the window.

3. Have you seen the real me.

4. Next time, won't you sing with me.

Daily Warm-Ups: Writing

38

An exclamation point indicates strong emotion.

It may be used at the end of a declarative statement or after an imperative (a request or an order)

Write a sentence ending with an exclamation point.

Then team up with a classmate. Read aloud your exclamation, with emotion. Have him or her answer back with an exclamation that fits the situation. Then reverse the process.

Now try the same exercise, but substitute periods for the exclamation points. How does this change the response from your partner?

39

Make a list of all the words you think of when you hear the word *Halloween*. Then reread your list and, using some of those words, describe a Halloween experience.

40

Insert a logical punctuation mark at the end of each sentence.

1. What a glorious day

2. Did he win the contest

3. The unknown player came from behind to beat the best player in the league

4. She didn't hear the results

5. Can it be true

41

i am sorry.

That sentence is fine if you're E. E. Cummings (a poet who often did not use capitals), and it's a common, if lazy, form used in e-mail, but in standard writing, you have to capitalize the word *I* and the first word of every sentence.

What else do you have to capitalize? List as many capitalization rules as you can.

42

In the paragraph below, indicate which letters should be capitalized by underlining them three times.

mr. jansen rode to the game on the bus with the team. he was not hopeful about their chances; the rival tigers were formidable opponents. the pittsfield team's quarterback, t. j. marks, was an all-star and was in fine form this season. still, mr. jansen's panthers had been doing well in practice. maybe the panthers would win the battle of the big cats!

43

© 2003 J. Weston Walch, Publisher

Sir Richard Steele once wrote, "Reading is to the mind what exercise is to the body." Write a similar saying about writing.

44

"'What is the use of a book,' thought Alice, 'without pictures or conversations?'"

—Lewis Carroll, *Alice's Adventures in Wonderland*

Alice likes her books with pictures—and dialogue. What does dialogue add to a book? What are books without dialogue like? Do you enjoy reading dialogue? Have you ever read dialogue that was not believable? How did that affect your reading of the story? Write your responses below.

45

Quotation marks are used to enclose a speaker's exact words. For example: *I said, "I'm going to school."* An indirect quotation, one that tells the substance of what someone said but not his or her exact words, does not call for quotation marks. For example: *He said that he was going to be late for school.*

Write a few lines of dialogue that you might hear in the hallway at school. Be sure to use quotation marks correctly.

Daily Warm-Ups: Writing

46

when do you use quotation marks, other than in direct quotations? Write a rule below, and give three examples.

47

In the following sentences, the words in parentheses are often misused in writing. Circle the correct word. If you are unsure of the answer, check a dictionary.

1. What is the right (number, amount) of flour to use in this recipe?

2. There are (less, fewer) freshmen this year than last.

3. Is this his (everyday, every day) routine?

4. Is everyone packed and (already, all ready) to go?

Now write a sentence for each of the words in parentheses that you did not circle.

48

Write an original sentence for each of the

commonly misused or confused words below.

stationary	ascent
stationery	assent
council	brake
counsel	break

49

Writing is, of course, a form of communication. One difference between written and spoken communication is that writing must be quite clear; when you read something, there is no body language to help you interpret a message, and no person in front of you to ask for clarification.

What information is missing from the telephone message below? Rewrite it with appropriate information.

> Sal,
>
> Some guy called. He wants you to call him back.
>
> Jon

Now list the types of information you should always include in a written telephone message.

50

Do you know how to write a business letter? Define each term relating to letter-writing below.

return address

salutation

body

closing

signature

© 2003 J. Weston Walch, Publisher

When writing letters, form is important. Do you know how to punctuate the following salutations and closings? Fill in the appropriate punctuation.

1. Dear Madam

2. Cordially

3. Sincerely

4. Love

5. Dear Lance

6. Your friend

7. Dear Mr. Alphonse

8. To whom it may concern

9. Forever yours

10. Dear Grammy

52

Write an invitation to an event for a character in a novel you have read. The event may be anything you choose, but it should have something to do with that character and the plot of the story. Remember to include the necessary information: type of event, name of person for whom the event is being held, time, date, place, and an R.S.V.P. line with a name and phone number for guests to respond to.

53

Write a letter of complaint to a company from

which you have purchased something. Remember, this is a formal letter, not an e-mail; standards must be followed. Write your letter below, including all the necessary parts of a letter. (Normally you would type your letter. Here, just handwrite it, but use the proper format.) In a letter of complaint, you should always tell the recipient what you expect him or her to do about the problem.

54

Write the advertising copy (the words of the ad) for an article of clothing people your age might want to buy. This is advertising, so you do not need to write in complete sentences—but you do need to get people's attention. Use specific words that will appeal to your audience.

Now write the ad copy for an article of clothing someone of your parents' generation would be interested in. How will the language you use differ from that used in your first ad? What traits or concerns will you appeal to this time? Share your ads with classmates.

55

A cinquain is a controlled form of poetry. It has five lines and it follows this pattern:

line 1 — one word that names the subject

line 2 — two words that describe the subject

line 3 — three words that tell about what the subject does

line 4 — four words that tell how you feel about the subject

line 5 — one word that renames the subject or sums up the poem

Write a cinquain about something you do outside of school.

56

"There is no greater agony than bearing an untold story inside you."

—Maya Angelou, in *Daily News*

How do you feel about this quotation? Do you feel that strongly about writing—or about anything else? Write your responses below.

Good writing is a skill to be learned and practiced. It is also a habit. To develop the writing habit, you need to write often.

Try a free writing exercise. Just write whatever comes into your head until your teacher tells you to stop. Do not worry about sense, spelling, punctuation, or mechanics. Just write. Go!

Daily Warm-Ups: Writing

58

Make a list of all the words you think of when you hear the phrase *extracurricular activities*. Then write a paragraph, using some of those words, explaining why you do or do not enjoy your extracurricular activities.

Think about a novel you have read that features a memorable character. Now write a letter of recommendation for that character, suggesting him or her for a particular job that you think is suitable. Remember to use proper business letter format.

60

A letter to the editor is an opinion letter a reader writes to be published in the newspaper. Letters to the editor are often about subjects that have been reported in the newspaper, or they are responses to another letter to the editor written by someone else.

Think about a current event from the news or at school. Write a letter to the editor about the issue. Letters to the editor are usually short—the newspaper wants to print several, not just one long one. Use proper business letter format, and use *Dear Editor* as your salutation.

61

Imagine that you need advice about something, and you do not want to ask your family or friends about it. Write a letter to advice columnist Pat Answer about your problem. Use proper letter format, and sign your letter with a pseudonym, or pen name, so that you can remain anonymous.

Now exchange letters with a classmate. As Pat, write a response to your classmate's letter.

Daily Warm-Ups: Writing

62

Alliteration is the repetition of an initial

sound, such as in *slithering snake* and *lonely, lingering light*. Alliteration is a sound device used to create a feeling or association. The s's in *slithering snake* are a drawn-out sound—and they mimic the sound the snake makes. The *l* sound in *lonely, lingering light* is a gentle sound, as calm as a fading sunset. Alliteration is often used in poetry, but it may be used in prose as well.

Think of some examples of alliteration you remember from your reading. Or make up some phrases using alliteration. What feelings or associations do the sounds create?

63

"It is the writer's privilege to help man endure by lifting his heart."

—William Faulkner, from a speech given upon receiving the Nobel Prize for Literature, 1950

What is your response to the quotation above? Does all literature lift the human heart? What does *lifting the human heart* mean to you?

64

Point of view is the perspective from which a story is told. The sentence *I went to the beach today* is written in the first person. The person telling the story is "I."

Imagine that you are your language arts or English teacher. Write a diary entry about what happened in school today. Remember to use "I."

65

© 2003 J. Weston Walch, Publisher

Imagine that you are a piece of equipment being used in a gym class. Write a few paragraphs about your day. Remember to use the first person "I." Share your writing with a classmate and see if she or he can guess what piece of equipment you are.

66

When writing in the first person, you

can explain and describe everything the narrator ("I") is thinking, feeling, and doing. This gives you the chance to really show one character. This point of view has limitations, however. With the first person, you cannot explain what other characters are thinking or feeling. You can only report what "I" can see. That means that if "I" is asleep while there is some action going on, the reader has to learn about it when the narrator does.

Another common point of view is the third person. This means that someone outside the story narrates it.

Think about the last three novels you read. From what point of view was each written? How did the point of view affect or limit the story?

67

Read the following news report about an accident:

This morning at 9:00, two cars collided on Main Street. A blue sedan driven by Tim Walker was stopped at the light at Main and Hudson streets. Marlene Hansen was traveling down Main Street when she slowed down to avoid a cat in the road. As Ms. Hansen accelerated, Mr. Walker hit her passenger side. No injuries were reported.

Imagine that you are Mr. Walker. Tell your side of the story, in the first person. Then imagine that you are Ms. Hansen, and tell your version of the story. When you have finished, reread the two eyewitness versions of the accident. Can they both be true? How does point of view affect even a "factual" account?

68

Imagine that you work in the advertising department of a book publisher. You are responsible for writing the back-cover copy—the blurbs—for young-adult novels.

Write a blurb that you think will appeal to young adults. You may write your blurb for an existing book that you have read, or make up a book to write about. Make your copy interesting, but don't give away too much of the story!

69

"In every man's [person's] writings, the character of the writer must lie recorded."

—Thomas Carlyle, *Goethe*

Respond to the quotation above, which was written in 1828. Do you agree or disagree? Why? Do you think the quotation applies today? Write your response and your reasons below.

Daily Warm-Ups: Writing

70

"The pen is mightier than the sword."

—Edward Bullwer Lytton, *Richelieu*

Respond to the quotation above. Do you agree or disagree? Are there circumstances in which it is true or untrue? Explain your ideas below.

"And were an epitaph to be my story

I'd have a short one ready for my own.
I would have written of me on my stone:
I had a lover's quarrel with the world."

—Robert Frost, "The Lesson for Today"

The quotation above refers to an epitaph, a saying that appears on one's gravestone. How would you like to be remembered? Write one sentence or phrase that tells something about your life. This would be permanent, so be sure you say what you mean, and say it well.

72

Write a motto or slogan for your school. Try to capture something unique or interesting about the school in your motto.

73

Make a list of all the words you think of when you hear the phrase *report card*. Then reread your list and sum up in a sentence the feelings *report card* brings up for you.

74

Ballads are a kind of song with a strong
narrative structure. They often tell a story in chronological order.
That is, they tell the events in the order that they occurred.

Write the words to a ballad about an event you have experienced
or witnessed. Write at least three verses, and include a refrain, or
repeated lines, between the verses. Be sure that the action of your
ballad is presented in chronological order.

75

© 2003 J. Weston Walch, Publisher

Make a list of all the words you think of when you hear the word *holiday*. Then write a paragraph, using some of those words, describing your associations with holidays.

76

An acrostic is a kind of poem that takes its structure from the letters of one word. To create an acrostic, write a word vertically down the left-hand side of a sheet of paper. Each letter of that word serves as the first letter of a line of poetry, and the poem's subject is the initial word. In this case, write an acrostic about winter.

W

I

N

T

E

R

77

"**The first** and most important thing of all, at least for writers today, is to strip language clean, to lay it bare down to the bone."

—Ernest Hemingway, quoted in *Paris Was Our Mistress* by Samuel Putnam

What does the quotation above suggest about word choice? What does it suggest about general versus specific words? Do you agree with Hemingway? Explain.

78

Daily Warm-Ups: Writing

There are many reasons to write. Below,

make a list of the reasons you write. Then rank them in order of
importance (to you) by numbering them, with 1 being the most
important. Compare your list with that of a classmate.

79

You may have heard of the writing process. Do you remember the steps? Write them down. Then explain what each step involves.

Do you follow the writing process for all your writing, or just certain types of writing? Explain.

80

Unless a specific writing topic is assigned, where do you get your ideas? Imagine that you have been given the broad topic of ecology to write about for science class. To come up with a narrower topic, you can try brainstorming. This means quickly writing down whatever comes into your head about the general topic. Go ahead and brainstorm about ecology until your teacher tells you time is up.

On another sheet of paper, group the words you brainstormed into categories. Is one category more full than others? Do you see a group of words clustered around one idea? Looking for patterns in a brainstormed list can help you choose a manageable topic that is interesting to you.

81

© 2003 J. Weston Walch, Publisher

After the prewriting steps of the writing
process, it is time to write your first draft. Write your definition of
first draft below. Then tell what your goal is in a first draft.

82

The word *revise* means literally "to look at again." When you revise a draft of an essay or composition, what kinds of things do you look for? Write them below.

83

When you revise, you look at your work with a fresh eye. Besides rereading, how else can you check your work for things that need to be changed?

84

Write an acrostic using the word below.

L

E

A

D

E

R

85

After an essay has been revised for organization, content, and style, you can deal with the mechanics. This step is proofreading.

Below are some common proofreading marks and their meanings.

delete, or take out ✍

capitalize ☰

make lowercase /

add what is written above or in the margin ∧

add a comma ⌃

add a period ⊙

86

Rewrite the paragraph below by following the proofreader's marks.

The /Tarantula is a ~~very interesting~~ creature ~~that is~~ unique in many ways. For one thing, the tarantula has claws at the end of͜of its eight legs. it also has fangs that stab from above, like a snake's, rather than from the sides, as most spiders' do. ~~Although a tarantula's venom can kill a small animal it can rarely kill a human being.~~ Besides its bite͜the͜has another defense: it can throw irritating hairs from its abdomen. these hairs sting and can even blind. Despite these fierce Characteristics, tarantulas are generally very gentle creatures⊙

(inserted above "of": each)
(inserted above "the": tarantula)

A story generally has three parts: a

beginning, a middle, and an end. An essay has three parts, too. Write them below. Then tell what kind of information you would include in each part.

87

When you get ready to write an essay, you need to decide who your audience is. In school, your audience is usually your teacher and perhaps your classmates. If you keep a portfolio or display your work in some way, you may have a wider audience.

Read the list of essay titles below. On the line, write who you think the target audience is for each one.

Daily Warm-Ups: Writing

1. "How to Write a Descriptive Essay" _____
_____

2. "Finding the Perfect Mate" _____

3. "Turn Your Old Barbies into Cash!" _____

4. "The Effect of Radiation Treatment on Stage 4 Lung Cancer Patients" _____

5. "Going to the Dentist" _____

6. "Social Security and You"_____

7. "Basic Bicycle Maintenance" _____

88

A writer intends to reach a particular audience. Answer the questions below about how the audience affects what and how a writer writes.

1. How does the audience affect the subject matter?

2. How does the audience affect vocabulary?

3. How does the audience affect writing style?

4. How does the audience affect the organization of the essay?

89

© 2003 J. Weston Walch, Publisher

Make a list of all the words you think of when you hear the word *adolescence*. Then write two paragraphs: one describing a generic adolescent, and one that tells about a real adolescent you know. Does the paragraph about the real person resemble the stereotype of an adolescent?

90

All writing has a purpose. Even writing for

pleasure has a purpose. In that case, the purpose is to give pleasure to the writer. Usually, though, a writer has a purpose related to an audience: he or she wants to communicate an idea and perhaps spur the audience to some kind of action.

One purpose for writing is to explain something. If you were to write an expository, or explanatory, essay, what kind of information would you need about your topic? Where might you find that information? Write your ideas below.

Type of information	Where to find it

91

Description can be a purpose for writing. When might description be a good type of writing to use? What kind of words would you probably use? How might you organize a descriptive essay? Write your ideas below.

92

Narrative writing means writing to tell a story. It does not have to be a fictional story; it may be the story of what happened during your summer vacation, for example. Narrative writing is usually told in chronological order—the order in which events actually occurred.

Read the list of events below. Number them from 1 to 5 to indicate the sequence in which you think they happened.

_____ The doctor gave the girl an inoculation.

_____ The little girl cried.

_____ The little girl had a doctor's appointment for a physical.

_____ The shot didn't hurt a bit!

_____ The little girl was scared when the doctor brought out a syringe.

93

The sequence of events or the order of steps in a

process can be very important. Some words that signal sequence are *first*, *second*, *third*, *then*, *next*, *finally*, *after*, and *before*.

In the paragraph below, the steps in the process are out of order. Rewrite the paragraph, correcting the sequence and adding sequence words where they are needed.

Rinse your mouth so that you do not swallow any toothpaste. Spend at least two minutes brushing all the surfaces of your teeth. Floss your teeth. Squeeze a dollop of fluoride toothpaste on the bristles of the toothbrush. Spit out the used toothpaste. Brush your tongue, too. Brush your teeth using up-and-down strokes.

94

Daily Warm-Ups: Writing

One purpose for writing is to persuade readers that your view is correct. This may lead the reader simply to agree with you, or it may prompt him or her to vote for a certain candidate, or to buy a certain product, or to change his or her behavior.

Think about the various types of reading you do outside the classroom. List the kinds of persuasive writing you have read.

What kind of language does this type of writing use? How do you feel when you read persuasive writing? Did any of the persuasive pieces that you listed try to get the reader to take some action?

95

© 2003 J. Weston Walch, Publisher

You have to decide how to organize any writing you do. Read the numbered topics and purposes below. Then choose a type of organization from the box that might make sense for that piece of writing. Write the letter of your choice on the line provided.

Possible organization patterns	
a. cause and effect	d. main idea and details
b. chronological order	e. opinion and supporting evidence
c. comparison and contrast	

Essay topics/purposes

_____ 1. give reasons for the start of World War II
_____ 2. tell how to make peanut butter cookies
_____ 3. explain why global warming is a problem
_____ 4. describe the effects of sun exposure on the skin
_____ 5. explain why soccer is better than football
_____ 6. tell about your visit to the Grand Canyon

Compare your choices with that of a classmate. Discuss any choices that differ.

One common organizational pattern

in writing is main idea and details. The paragraph below has plenty of details. The main idea is understood but never directly stated. Read the paragraph. Then write the main idea in one sentence.

The leaves are breathtaking: red, yellow, orange, and still a hint of green. The changing hues are a sign of impending death, but the sight is still beautiful. The air is crisp, just cool enough for a jacket, but not cold enough for gloves. Farm stands have an ample supply of seasonal produce, such as squash, pumpkin, and Indian corn. Pick-your-own-apples signs sprout all over New England, inviting you to pluck the fruit right from the trees. I love this season!

97

When you compare two things, you tell how they are alike. When you contrast them, you tell how they are different. In what type of situation would you want to compare two things? In what situation would you want to contrast two things? List as many ideas as you can below. Then share your list with a classmate and discuss what you wrote.

98

When you compare and contrast two things, you want to be sure your audience knows what you are doing. You don't want your readers to think you are comparing your favorite candidate to a crook, for example.

Write some comparison words that would link two things that are similar. Then write some contrast words that would emphasize how two things are different.

Share your lists with the class. Did most people have similar lists?

99

Make a list of all the words you think of when you hear the word *vacation*. Then write a paragraph, using some of those words, contrasting school days and vacation.

100

An analogy is a set of paired words that share a similar relationship. *Sad is to happy as up is to down* is an analogy. Analogies are often written in a particular form using colons. For example, *sad : happy :: up : down*.

The examples above happen to have an antonym relationship, but there are many other possibilities, such as cause and effect, an object and its use, or a part to its whole.

Complete the analogy below.

communication : _____ :: _____ : _____

101

© 2003 J. Weston Walch, Publisher

In a letter to Lady Beaumont in 1807, the poet William Wordsworth wrote, "Every great and original writer . . . must himself create the taste by which he is to be relished."

What do you think Wordsworth meant? What does this quotation suggest about writing styles?

102

Many written pieces, including letters to the editor, book and movie reviews, and newspaper editorials, are organized as opinions supported by reasons. Sometimes it can be difficult to tell when someone is giving an opinion versus stating a fact. Certain words let you know that what is written is an opinion.

Can you think of some words that signal an opinion? Write as many as you can below. A few possibilities have been given to get you started.

I think . . .

In my opinion . . .

103

A book review or a movie review is often an opinion supported by reasons. Write a book review or a movie review, being sure to state your opinion and give at least three supporting reasons.

Daily Warm-Ups: Writing

104

Brainstorm words you think of when you see the phrase *civil rights*. Then use those words to write a free-verse poem about the subject. A free-verse poem does not follow a set pattern or rhyme scheme.

105

Imagine that you did not turn in an English paper on time. You now have an additional assignment: write a paper about why you did not write your paper. Imagine that you are going to organize that paper following a cause-and-effect pattern. Fill in the flowchart below with the causes and effects you will include in your paper. Add and remove boxes and arrows as needed.

106

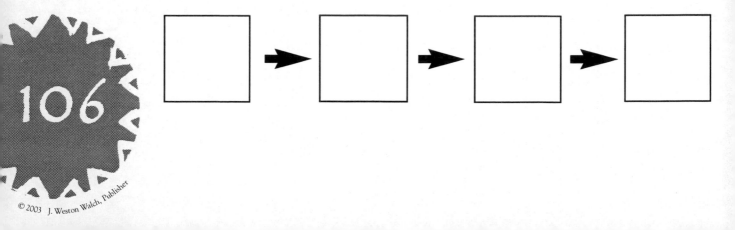

A writer wants to make things clear for her or his audience. Using signal words or clue words helps the reader understand what the writer is communicating.

The cause-and-effect pattern of organization can be signaled by certain words. How many can you think of? Write them below. Then compare your list with that of a classmate.

107

Chronological order means "time order," or the
order in which events happen. If you are going to write about
something in chronological order, sometimes a timeline can help.

Imagine that you have been asked to write about a typical school
day. Fill in the timeline below with times and activities to help you
organize your imaginary essay.

108

As with other ways to organize writing, a chronological order pattern is signaled or emphasized by certain words. One way to tell the reader when events happen is to give actual times: *At three o'clock, the last bell of the school day rang.*

Besides specific times, can you think of any words that clue the reader in about the order of events? Write them below. A few possibilities have been given to get you started.

first

then

before

109

What does celebrating Black History Month mean to you? Write a paragraph about what you would like to learn and why.

110

Sentences can be classified in various ways.

When you group sentences by structure, there are four kinds. Can you name them? Write them below. Then give an example of each.

111

To keep your writing fresh, it is generally a

good idea to vary sentence structure. Too many short, choppy simple sentences or too many long, complicated complex sentences can bore or confuse the reader.

Rewrite the paragraph below by combining or breaking up the sentences.

Travis Pastrana is a dirt bike racer. He is also a stunt rider. He competes in televised competitions. Riders launch off a jump. Then they take their hands or feet off the bike. Then they twist themselves into different positions. Travis Pastrana is a champion on the track. He is also a champion in the air.

112

The setting is the time and place of a story. It often sets a mood for the whole story. *It was a dark and stormy night* has become a clichéd opening for mystery and thriller stories.

Think about setting and genre, or writing type. If you were going to write historical fiction, what setting might you choose? Write the time period, the climate, the style of dress of your characters, and other clues that reveal your setting.

113

Plot means the events of a fictional story. Most plots include some kind of conflict, or problem, that the characters have to deal with. For each type of conflict below, invent a specific conflict that you think could be the center of an interesting story.

Types of conflict	Specific conflict ideas
person against person	
person against himself or herself	
person against nature	
person against technology	

114

Write a haiku about the end of winter.

115

Characters are people who appear in a story. Read the paragraph below. Pay attention to how the main character is characterized.

After a few minutes of fuming, May Ling lifted her square chin to look in the mirror. She blinked with surprise at her flushed face. She recombed her part so that it neatly bisected her dark head. She took a deep breath, counted to five, and exhaled. She pulled her precious books out from under the bed where she had kicked them and set them squarely on the corner of her desk. After choosing a color-coded mechanical pencil from the desk drawer, she began brainstorming about the language arts paper that was due next week.

Now describe May Ling. What does she look like? What are some personality traits? What is important to her?

116

One way to characterize a character is to show how she or he behaves. In movies, writers cannot say what anyone is like; they show it with images of the character doing something. Think about a character from a favorite movie. Imagine that you have been hired to write a book based on the movie. Write a character sketch, capturing the qualities of that character in words.

117

Write a few lines of dialogue that reveal

what someone you know is like. Don't use the person's name.
You may want to include expressions that person often uses and
subjects that person is interested in and likely to really talk about.
Then share your dialogue with a classmate. Ask her or him to tell
you what kind of person your character seems to be. Did your
partner understand what you were trying to show?

Daily Warm-Ups: Writing

118

Dialogue tells about character and plot

not only through what the characters say, but also how they say it.

"That paper is on fire!" yelled the fire chief, pointing to the stack of newspapers in the recycling center.

"That paper is on fire!" trumpeted the reporter after his article broke all records for drawing letters to the editor.

"That paper is on fire," explained the safety instructor as he gave the class another handout.

In the examples above the dialogue is the same, but the emotion and emphasis behind it changes. Write five lines of dialogue (they do not all have to be the same) using different words to show *how* a character says something.

119

The pairs of words below are often

confused. Use each word in a sentence to show that you know
its correct meaning and usage. If you do not know the difference
between the words, look them up in a dictionary.

imply
infer

formally
formerly

perquisite
prerequisite

120

"If you would not be forgotten, as soon as you are rotten, either write things worth reading, or do things worth the writing."

—Benjamin Franklin

What does this quotation suggest about the permanence of the written word? What is your response to the quotation?

121

Imagine that a new student has just asked you
for directions to a room in your school. Write out the directions,
using order words to make the directions clear.

122

Imagine that you are on the committee

that is compiling a handbook for new students. You have been assigned to write the "welcome" letter at the front. You want to put new students at ease and help them enjoy their new school. Write your letter below.

123

Write the lyrics for a song about test-taking. Set your words to the tune of a well-known song ("Twinkle, Twinkle, Little Star," or "Old MacDonald Had a Farm," for example). You may want to share your song with the class.

Daily Warm-Ups: Writing

124

There are many overused and tired—some even say dead—words. Such words have been used so often that they no longer hold any real meaning. How many overused words can you list? Write them below. A few words have been given to get you started.

Overused Words

great

nice

125

One way to make your writing interesting is to avoid overused words and to use fresh, vivid ones instead. Rewrite the following paragraph, replacing the overused words with more vibrant ones.

Sam and I went to the concert last night. It was great. The music was really loud. The band was great. Sam's a good guy. We do fun things together.

126

Strong verbs are particularly important in writing. They can really energize your writing and keep your reader interested.

For each verb below, think of a strong, specific verb you could use instead. A few examples have been given to get you started.

Walk	Say	Look	Think
saunter	retort	glare	ponder

127

© 2003 J. Weston Walch, Publisher

Think about a book you enjoyed reading, for school or on your own. Write a letter from one character to another. Then write a reply from the second character to the first. Stay true to the characters and the way they would speak and write, based on what you have learned about them in the novel.

128

Write an opinion article about an event that occurred in a book you have read. Your audience is made up of the characters in the book.

129

Do you have a favorite author? He or she may write fiction, nonfiction, or journalistic pieces. Tell the story of a day in your life in the style of that author. If you don't have a favorite author, write in the style of the author of the last book you read.

130

Daily Warm-Ups: Writing

"It's never to late—in literature or in life—to revise."

—Nancy Thayer

Write your response to the above quotation. What does it say about the importance of revising? What does it say about the privilege of revising?

131

Sometimes when you are writing an essay,

you find yourself repeating the same word. This may be because it is a comfortable word for you, or because it is the subject of your paper. If you can, however, you should try to vary your vocabulary so that your reader is not bored.

One way to vary vocabulary is to use synonyms, or words that mean nearly the same thing.

For each word listed, write two synonyms you could use in its place.

Study	Research	Write	Answer

Choose a specific word from the box below to replace each underlined general word in the paragraph. You may use words of your own if you prefer. Rewrite the paragraph with your choices.

flew	sprinted	hurtled	wobbled
strolled	grabbed	inched	zoomed
lurched	snatched	crawled	whizzed
rolled	loped	gathered	sped

Beatriz <u>ran</u> to the window. The bus had just <u>come</u> to a stop. She <u>picked up</u> her lunch, <u>picked up</u> her coat, and <u>ran</u> out the door. Just as she <u>went</u> around the corner, the bus <u>drove</u> away.

133

Do you know what the 5 W's and 1 H are? They are the keys to good journalistic writing. Write what the letters stand for below.

W

W

W

W

W

H

134

Journalists strive to tell factual information in an interesting way. One way to spark interest is to write an interesting headline. Think about a novel you have read recently for a class. Choose three events from that book. Write an attention-getting headline for a story about each event. Remember, a headline should capture the main idea of a story.

135

Think about the plot of a novel you have read. List some of the cause-effect relationships in the book.

136

"Frothy eloquence neither convinces nor satisfies me. I am from Missouri. You have got to show me."

—Willard Duncan Vandiver, from a speech at a naval banquet, 1899

The speaker of the words above may not have believed what people say just because they say it; they would have to prove their point. What kind of information would you include in a persuasive essay if this person was the intended audience? What kind of information would be most convincing to this person?

137

Setting is the time and place of a story. One mistake that sometimes spoils a setting is the appearance of an anachronism. An anachronism is something that is out of its time. For example, a car driving through the countryside to announce the coming of British troops during the American Revolution would be an anachronism.

Write a scene containing an anachronism that makes the setting seem false.

138

"Poetry is the search for the inexplicable."

—Wallace Stevens, *Opus Posthumous*, 1957

Write your response to the quotation. How can poetry be a search?
How can poetry be used to explain the unexplainable?

139

Poetry is a condensed form of writing. It packs
a lot of meaning into very few words.

Free verse is poetry that does not follow a fixed pattern of syllables or rhyme. It is poetry rather than prose because it does not necessarily follow grammatical and punctuation conventions, and it is very economical. It often does use other poetic devices, such as alliteration, simile, and metaphor.

Write a free verse poem about an important event in your life.

Daily Warm-Ups: Writing

140

Write an interesting setting for a short story.

Switch papers with a classmate. Write a very short story (three to five paragraphs) using the setting your partner listed.

141

"**A powerful agent** is the right word. Whenever we come upon one of those intensely right words in a book or a newspaper the resulting effect is physical as well as spiritual, and electrically prompt."

—Mark Twain, *Essay on William Dean Howells*, 1906

Have you ever had the experience of finding or reading the "right word"? If so, describe how you felt and the context of the word. If not, explain how you feel when you cannot find the right word, or when you read something that contains poor word choices.

142

Imagine that you are doing a research project about students' attitudes toward writing. Write four questions you would ask. Be sure to make your questions open-ended; that is, make sure they require more than a yes or no answer.

After you have written your survey questions, form a group with three or four classmates and informally discuss and answer the group's questions.

143

Identifying and considering the audience is

an important part of the writing process. Imagine that as a service project, you are going to work with a younger student at the elementary school who needs help with writing. Write the steps of the writing process for a third-grader.

144

Have you ever experienced "writer's block," or the inability to get started writing? Write about that experience and how you overcame it. If you have not experienced writer's block, think about how you might jump-start your writing if you were stuck. Write your ideas below.

145

Do a free-association activity using the word below. Then share your writing with a classmate and discuss similarities and differences.

CREATIVITY

146

Daily Warm-Ups: Writing

Imagine that you have worked on an essay and are ready to share it with others. Besides presenting your work as a composition or paper, how else might you publish it? List some ideas below.

147

Sometimes characters in fiction have

interesting names. The names may tell about a personality trait, or just have an interesting sound.

Create and describe three characters who will appear in a short story. The story may be of any genre. Then write an interesting name for each character.

148

It is sometimes said that truth is stranger than fiction. Write about something strange but true that you experienced or heard about. Since this is factual reporting, use the 5 W's and 1 H.

149

Legends are stories passed down through generations that have a kernel of truth to them but that have been embellished. Are there any legends about the place where you live? If so, write one below. If not, write about another legend you have heard. Then write what you think the kernel of truth might be at the center of the story.

Daily Warm-Ups: Writing

150

Daily Warm-Ups: Writing

If you want to convince someone of something, which phrases below would be useful? Put a checkmark by your choices.

_____ I guess

_____ perhaps

_____ certainly

_____ as I see it

_____ the evidence shows

_____ therefore

_____ without a doubt

Write two more strong, convincing words that you could use in a persuasive essay.

151

© 2003 J. Weston Walch, Publisher

Rewrite a familiar fairy tale to make it in some way surprising.

152

Daily Warm-Ups: Writing

An analogy is a set of paired words that share a similar relationship. Complete the analogy below.

words : _____ :: _____ : _____

© 2003 J. Weston Walch, Publisher

Imagine that you are tutoring ounger students about writing. Write a list of at least three things they should do if they are asked to offer feedback on a classmate's writing.

154

Imagine that you have been assigned to write a report entitled "The Economy of Blahblah," a topic about which you know very little. Below, brainstorm a list of sources you might turn to for information. Then share your list with a classmate.

155

Create a cause-and-effect chart about a science experiment you have done or seen. Then use your chart to write a paragraph explaining the experiment.

156

Write a short letter to the principal about something disturbing that happened at school and what action you would like to see taken. The incident may be real or imaginary. This letter is a business letter and should be written in the proper format and style. Then write a friendly letter to a friend or relative about the same incident. How are the words and tone of the two letters different?

157

Imagine that you are starting a writer's group at school. Write a motto for the group. Share your motto with classmates. Did all of the mottoes focus on the same aspect of writing, or was there a range of ideas?

158

Write a topic that could be used as a prompt for a short persuasive essay. Then exchange papers with a classmate and write the essay using his or her prompt. You will have only five minutes to write your essay. Remember that organization is important.

© 2003 J. Weston Walch, Publisher

An analogy is a set of paired words that share a similar relationship. Complete the analogy below.

preparation : _____ :: _____ : _____

160

A sentence may be written in the active voice or in the passive voice. In the active voice, the subject does something. In the passive voice, something is done to or by the subject.

Active voice: Mariah wrote the report about swimming with dolphins.

Passive voice: The report about swimming with dolphins was written by Mariah.

Writers are often advised to use the active voice, but sometimes the passive voice is preferable (reread this sentence). When might the passive voice be a better choice than the active voice?

161

Several sentences below are in the passive voice. Rewrite the paragraph so that most of the sentences are in the active voice. Keep the passive voice when it is a better choice.

Jake was surprised by the storm. He was awakened by the sound of high winds, and he was startled by the crash of a tree in the street. Its branches were strewn all over the neighborhood. Some parked cars had been blanketed by leaves. Windows in the building across the street had been shattered by the wind.

162

Write a few paragraphs about your favorite author.

Explain why you like this person's writing.

163

Write a paragraph explaining where you get most of your news (television, car radio, newspaper, and Internet are possibilities). Be sure to tell why you use that form of communication.

164

Daily Warm-Ups: Writing

List as many kinds of nonfiction writing as you can.

Then compare your list with those of classmates.

Do you prefer doing creative writing or nonfiction writing? Why?

166

How do you feel when you receive a letter in the mailbox? Do you feel the same when you receive an e-mail message? If you do feel different, why do you prefer one over the other?

167

Reading and writing are closely linked. How do you think one affects the other?

168

"He spoke with a certain what-is-it in his voice, and I could see that, if not actually disgruntled, he was far from being gruntled."

—P. G. Wodehouse, *The Code of the Woosters*

Sometimes it is hard to find just the right word to describe something. Make up your own words or phrases to describe the following things.

a cake that has gone stale

a dull day

a teacher who talks on and on

a hilarious television show

your favorite CD

169

Write a cinquain about the American flag or another
national symbol.

170

When your parents or other caretakers were in school, they may not have learned about the writing process. Write and explain the steps of the writing process so they will understand it.

171

You are probably familiar with rhymes. They are used in songs, in poems, in nursery rhymes, in games, in advertising, and elsewhere. *Rhyme scheme* refers to the pattern of rhyme in a poem. For example, the limerick below follows a rhyme scheme of *aabba*, in which the first, second, and last lines (the *a* lines) rhyme, and the third and fourth (the *b* lines) rhyme.

A family once lived in a shoe.
The children were always quite blue.
"To live in this stink,
We at least need a sink
To get rid of this shoe's P-U!"

Write the lyrics of a verse of a song you like. Then label the lines to tell what the rhyme scheme is.

172

"Would I had phrases that are not known, utterances that are strange, in new language that has not been used, free from repetition, not an utterance which has grown stale, which men of old have spoken."

—Egyptian inscription recorded at the time of the invention of writing

People have been striving for originality and individuality in their writing for a long time! What is your response to the quotation? How does it make you feel?

173

Subjects and verbs must agree.

This does not mean that they must share an opinion. It means that singular and plural subjects take different verb forms. Circle the correct verb in each sentence below.

1. Henry (go/goes) to the library Wednesday afternoons.

2. Isabelle (chooses/choose) to spend her time reading.

3. Betsy and Andrew always (try/tries) their best in phys ed.

4. Austin and Justine (does/do) not seem to care much about their grades.

5. Drew (helps/help) at the soup kitchen on Saturdays.

Write two rules for when to use a semicolon. Then insert semicolons if and where they are needed below.

1. The pure sciences are very interesting for some however, the applied sciences are more useful.

2. It took all day to complete the competition because I had to do a written test with multiple-choice, short-answer, and essay questions run, bike, and swim two miles each and pass a practical lifesaving exam covering first aid, CPR, and the Heimlich maneuver.

3. The teacher announced that students would be divided into the following groups of three: Mary, Janie, Tomas, Sophie, Liza, Tammi, and Lee Ann, Linda, and Rodney.

175

Imagine that you would like to celebrate something for which there is no holiday. Write a paragraph explaining why you think this event deserves a holiday.

Daily Warm-Ups: Writing

176

Write a diary entry describing the stress you feel during tests and how you deal with it. Share your entry with a classmate. Discuss your coping strategies.

177

Choose a book you have read that contains a conflict between two people. As the protagonist (the main character), write a letter to the antagonist (the person who opposes the main character) suggesting a way the two of you can resolve the conflict.

178

Parallel construction refers to making sure you structure all the parts of a sentence similarly so that it flows and does not confuse the reader.

Correct: He asked for his check, paid the server, and left the restaurant.

Not correct: He decided to write the letter, fax it, asked his mother for directions, and left.

Correct the sentences below so that they show parallel construction.

1. By doing your homework, hard work, and studying, you will succeed.

2. It is not only disobeying the speed limit that is the problem but also a failure to use directionals when turning.

3. She was nervous about the test, so she stayed up late to review, study, and wrote notes.

179

Write a cinquain about the last day of school.

180

1–4. Answers will vary.

5. The parts of speech are noun, pronoun, verb, adjective, adverb, conjunction, preposition, and interjection. Examples will vary.

6. Lists will vary. Including proper nouns makes writing realistic and gives readers more concrete images.

7. I/I; he; she; he. Other answers will vary but may include that the correct pronoun sounds right when read aloud. One way to check a pronoun is to plug in the noun it is replacing to see if it makes sense.

8. Answers may vary a bit, but should be close to the following: Esmeralda loved playing her clarinet. Although she was talented, Esmeralda lacked the discipline to practice every day. Her dream was to play professionally. Esmeralda's parents worried that their daughter would not reach her goal if she did not work harder.

9–16. Answers will vary.

17. 1(a); 2(a); 3(a); 4(a)

18. Answers may vary, but the following are possibilities: 1. While they were driving to the store, the baby spit up on her dad's jacket. *or* The baby spit up on her dad's jacket on the ride to the store. 2. Blinded by the storm, the skiers swooshed past the lodge. *or* The skiers, blinded by the storm, swooshed past the lodge. 3. First he said he would go; then he changed his mind and stayed home. 4. Before the doctor finished her rounds, Suzanne asked her for some advice. *or* Before Suzanne finished her rounds, she asked the doctor for some advice.

19–26. Answers will vary.

27. Answers will vary. Some students may point to advertising as a source of hyperbole, or people trying to impress others.

28. Answers will vary.

29. Answers will vary. Understatement is sometimes used to be humorous. It is also used to downplay something unpleasant.

30. Answers will vary.

31. Answers will vary. Some students may suggest that allusions can serve as a kind of shorthand, making a connection for the reader without spelling it out.

They also may help the reader connect with the writer, feeling that they have knowledge in common or share "inside" information.

32. Answers will vary.

33. 1(a); 2(c); 3(e); 4(i); 5(g); 6(h); 7(d); 8(b); 9(j); 10(f)

34. Answers may include some of the following: use a comma between items in a series, after a direct address, after the greeting and closing of a letter, after an introductory word or phrase, to set off parenthetical phrases, to set off an appositive, to set off degrees or other modifiers after a person's name, between the city and state in addresses, and to separate clauses. Examples will vary.

35. Once in a while, Sheila went to the movies alone. She didn't have to share her popcorn, she didn't have to shush her companion, and she didn't have to debate which movie to see. On the other hand, there was also no one to poke in the ribs when a character said something funny, and there was no one to explain when something unexpected happened. She wasn't sure which way was better, but she loved going to the movies.

36. Answers may include some of the following: use a period at the end of a declarative statement, after imperatives (gentle requests), after abbreviations, after initials, and when writing dollar amounts. Examples will vary.

37. 1. Take W. River St. to Overpass Rd., and turn left at the first set of lights. 2. Miss Washington is my piano teacher this year. 3. Dr. Ahmed ordered some tests to be done at the lab on E. 42nd Street. 4. It's impossible that M. L. Burns is Melissa Lou Burns. 5. I have a copy of *The Elements of Style* by William Strunk, Jr., and E. B. White.

38. Change the period to a question mark in items 2, 3, and 4.

39. Answers will vary.

40. Answers will vary.

41. 1 ! or . 2 ? 3 ! or . 4 . or ! or ? 5 ?

42. Answers will vary but may include some of the following: capitalize proper nouns and proper adjectives; the titles of books, long plays, and movies; acronyms; certain institutions; and the word Bible

when referring to the sacred book. Examples will vary.

43. Mr. Jansen rode to the game on the bus with the team. He was not hopeful about their chances; the rival Tigers were formidable opponents. The Pittsfield team's quarterback, T. J. Marks, was an all-star and was in fine form this season. Still, Mr. Jansen's Panthers had been doing well in practice. Maybe the Panthers would win the battle of the big cats!

44–46. Answers will vary.

47. Answers will vary but may include some of the following: use quotation marks around titles of articles, poems, short plays, and television episodes; and for emphasis of a term. Examples will vary.

48. 1. amount; 2. fewer; 3. everyday; 4. all ready. Sentences will vary.

49. Answers will vary.

50. Messages will vary. Types of information to include are the name of the person calling, the message, any action to be taken, the time of the call, and the name of the person who took the call.

51. Return address: the name and address of the sender; salutation: the greeting or "Dear" line; body: the main part of the letter; closing: the "good-bye" line (such as Sincerely, Yours truly, Cordially); signature: the sender's handwritten name

52. 1. Dear Madam: 2. Cordially, 3. Sincerely, 4. Love, 5. Dear Lance, 6. Your friend, 7. Dear Mr. Alphonse: 8. To whom it may concern: 9. Forever yours, 10. Dear Grammy,

53–57. Answers will vary.

58. NOTE: This is a timed exercise. Allow five minutes for free writing.

59–79. Answers will vary.

80. Briefly, the writing process steps are prewriting, drafting, revising, and publishing. A more detailed list might include a breakdown of prewriting steps (brainstorming, narrowing a topic, determining audience, defining purpose), followed by drafting, revising, editing, proofreading, and publishing.

81. Answers will vary.

82. Answers will vary, but students may say that the first draft is for getting ideas on paper without worrying about mechanics.

83. Answers will vary but may include clear organization, sense, clarity, and correctness of information.

84. Answers will vary. Possibilities include: reading your work aloud to yourself, reading aloud to a peer or someone else, or giving it to someone else to read.

85. Answers will vary.

86. The tarantula is a creature unique in many ways. For one thing, the tarantula has claws at the end of each of its eight legs. It also has fangs that stab down from above, like a snake's, rather than from the sides, as most spiders' do. Besides its bite, the tarantula has another defense: it can throw irritating hairs from its abdomen. These hairs sting and can even blind. Despite these fierce characteristics, tarantulas are generally very gentle creatures.

87. An essay usually has an introduction, a body, and a conclusion. The introduction sets up the essay and usually contains the thesis statement. The body supports the thesis statement. The conclusion sums up the essay and often restates the thesis statement.

88. Answers may vary, but the following are likely possibilities. 1. middle-school and high-school students; 2. adults looking for a life partner; 3. girls or women (perhaps also boys and men) who have kept dolls from childhood; 4. doctors or other health professionals; 5. young children who haven't visited the dentist before; 6. older people who need information about Social Security; 7. people who have not been responsible for regular care of a bicycle, such as a child.

89. Answers will vary but may include some of the following ideas. 1. The subject matter will have to be something that appeals to the audience and that the audience can understand. 2. The vocabulary has to be at an appropriate level for the audience: simple for young children or people unfamiliar with something, and more complex or containing jargon for people who are experts. 3. You would probably use shorter and fewer sentences for

children, and longer, more complex constructions for adults. 4. You might want to use a predictable main idea/details pattern for people without a lot of background, and more sophisticated organization for people who will not have trouble understanding the basic ideas.

90–92. Answers will vary.

93. 4, 3, 1, 5, 2

94. Answers will vary. The following is a possibility: First squeeze a dollop of fluoride toothpaste on the bristles of the toothbrush. Next, brush your teeth using up-and-down strokes. Spend at least two minutes brushing all the surfaces of your teeth. Brush your tongue, too. Then, spit out the used toothpaste. Rinse your mouth so that you do not swallow any toothpaste. Finally, floss your teeth.

95. Answers will vary.

96. Answers may vary, but the following are likely possibilities. 1(a); 2(b); 3(a) or (e); 4(a); 5(c) or (e); 6(b) or (d)

97. Answers will vary. The following is one possibility: Fall is a wonderful time of year in New England.

98. Answers will vary.

99. Answers will vary. Possibilities include the following: Comparison words: similarly, like, as, in the same way, just as, both. Contrast words: unlike, on the other hand, this is not the case, different, differently.

100–102. Answers will vary.

103. Answers will vary. Possibilities include: I believe, it seems to me, I feel.

104–106. Answers will vary.

107. Answers will vary. Possibilities include: because, since, then, after that, this led to that, as a result, as a consequence.

108. Answers will vary.

109. Answers will vary. Possibilities include: next, finally, after, afterward, during, at the beginning, at the end, second, third, simultaneously.

110. Answers will vary.

111. The four types are: simple, compound, complex, compound-complex. Examples will vary.

112. Answers will vary. The following is one possibility: Travis Pastrana is both a dirt bike racer and stunt

rider. He competes in televised competitions. First, riders launch off a jump. Then they take their hands or feet off the bike and twist themselves into different positions. Travis Pastrana is a champion both on the track and in the air.

113.   Answers will vary.

114.   Answers will vary.

115.   Answers will vary. Students may need to be reminded of the haiku form. See warm-up 2 for an explanation.

116.   Answers may vary. May Ling has dark hair and a square chin. She is not usually flushed. She seems to be neat, organized, and methodical. She cares enough about neatness to arrange things on her desk, and she gets a head start on homework.

117–133. Answers will vary.

134.   The five W's are who, what, where, when, and why. The H is how.

135.   Answers will vary.

136.   Answers will vary.

137–150. Answers will vary.

151.   Certainly, surely, the evidence shows, therefore, without a doubt. Students' words will vary.

152–158. Answers will vary.

159.   NOTE: This is a timed exercise. Give students five minutes to write after they have exchanged papers. Answers will vary.

160.   Answers will vary.

161.   Answers will vary. Possibilities include: when the name of the subject is unknown, or when the subject is unimportant compared to the action.

162–169. Answers will vary.

170.   Answers will vary. Students may need to be reminded of the cinquain form. See warm-up 56 for an explanation.

171–173. Answers will vary.

174.   1. goes; 2. chooses; 3. try; 4. do; 5. helps

175.   Use a semicolon to separate items in a list when commas are already used and to join two independent clauses without a conjunction. 1. The pure sciences are very interesting for some; however, the applied sciences are more useful. 2. It

took all day to complete the competition because I had to do a written test with multiple-choice, short-answer, and essay questions; run, bike, and swim two miles each; and pass a practical life-saving exam covering first aid, CPR, and the Heimlich maneuver. 3. The teacher announced that students would be divided into the following groups of three: Mary, Janie, Tomas; Sophie, Liza, Tammi; and Lee Ann, Linda, and Rodney.

176–178. Answers will vary.

179. Answers will vary. Some possibilities follow. 1. By doing your homework, working hard, and studying, you will succeed. 2. It is not only disobeying the speed limit that is the problem but also failing to use directionals when turning. 3. She was nervous about the test, so she stayed up late to review, study, and write notes.

180. Answers will vary. Students may need to be reminded of the cinquain form. See warm-up 56 for an explanation.

Turn downtime into learning time!

Other books in the

Daily *Warm-Ups* series:

- Algebra
- Analogies
- Biology
- Critical Thinking
- Earth Science
- Geography
- Geometry
- Journal Writing
- Poetry
- Pre-Algebra
- Shakespeare
- Spelling & Grammar
- U.S. History
- Test-Prep Words
- Vocabulary
- World History